GUY FAW

AND THE GUNPOWDE

Peter Brimacombe

GUY FAWKES is remembered every year throughout the nation, yet achieved
nothing. Branded one of the greatest villains of all time, he is synonymous
with a spectacular crime that he neither led nor actually committed. Fawkes
was not the instigator of the Gunpowder Plot, yet he holds a place in history
as the man responsible.

He and his fellow plotters were fanatical amateurs, obsessed by their beliefs,
caught up in a sinister world of intrigue, treachery and betrayal, full of spies,
double agents and informers controlled by King James's veteran chief minister,
the shrewdly manipulative Earl of Salisbury.

The heady Elizabethan days that followed the defeat of the Spanish Armada had
gone. A new century brought England a new king, James I, imported from Scotland.
His experiences had created a suspicious nature, and under his rule the atmosphere
in England darkened. Among other concerns, he and his men were preoccupied by
the threat to national security posed by Catholic conspiracy. Two recent plots
against the king had been ruthlessly terminated by torture and the scaffold.

Conspirators such as Robert Catesby, Tom Winter and Jack Wright were
known suspects, already under surveillance. Soon Guy Fawkes's name also reached
Salisbury's ear. Salisbury, a fervent Protestant, almost certainly saw the proposed
Gunpowder Plot as an opportunity to discredit the Catholic cause.
Guy Fawkes was soon to become a doomed man.

Early Life

Guy Fawkes was born in York in 1570. Today plaques in High Petergate and Stonegate, in the shadow of York Minster, mark the vicinity of the house where he is thought to have lived with his parents, Edward and Edith Fawkes. His mother came from a Catholic family yet his father was Protestant, so Fawkes was baptized in the nearby Anglican church of St Michael-le-Belfrey. Fawkes's father died when he was eight and his mother subsequently married a Catholic. He also came under strong Catholic influence at the school he attended, St Peter's, York, where pupils included the brothers John (Jack) and Christopher (Kit) Wright, later to become fellow conspirators in the Gunpowder Plot. The school still exists; its most notorious pupil has been described by a modern-day head boy as 'not an ideal role model'.

In the early 1590s, after converting to Catholicism, Fawkes went to Flanders where for more than a decade he fought for the Spanish army in the long-running war against the Protestant Dutch. Changing his name to the Spanish style 'Guido', he later acquitted himself with valour in the regiment of Sir William Stanley, an officer who had originally served in Queen Elizabeth I's army under the Earl of Leicester. It was during his military service that Fawkes learned how to ignite gunpowder by setting and firing a 'slow train'. His expertise was to shape his destiny.

ABOVE AND RIGHT: *Fawkes's birthplace was actually somewhere between High Petergate (above) and Stonegate (right).*

Fawkes was tall and powerfully built with thick reddish brown hair, a fashionably flowing moustache and bushy auburn beard. Contemporaries described him as courageous, cheerful and intelligent with great resolution. Yet reputedly he was very devout, which could not be said of every soldier at the time.

Although, technically, Fawkes was a hired mercenary fighting for a foreign army in a foreign land, he saw himself very differently: as a latter-day crusader, fighting not for a country but for his God, a staunch Catholic believing totally in the justice of his cause. This conviction endured, regardless of circumstance, until his violent death.

A fellow soldier, the veteran Welshman Hugh Owen, introduced Fawkes to Thomas Winter who, after the war, in early 1604 took him to London to meet the charismatic Robert Catesby – who happened to be assembling a squad to blow the King of England to kingdom come.

ABOVE: *The entrance to St Peter's, the school in York which Guy Fawkes attended. Here Fawkes first met the brothers Jack and Kit Wright, who were destined to join him in the Gunpowder Plot.*

St Michael-le-Belfrey, York, the church where Guy Fawkes was baptized a Protestant, in the shadow of York Minster and close to the house where he lived as a child.

Catholicism in England

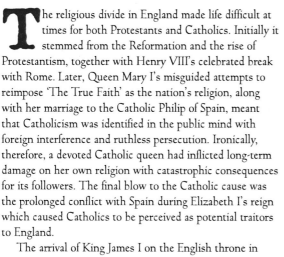

The religious divide in England made life difficult at times for both Protestants and Catholics. Initially it stemmed from the Reformation and the rise of Protestantism, together with Henry VIII's celebrated break with Rome. Later, Queen Mary I's misguided attempts to reimpose 'The True Faith' as the nation's religion, along with her marriage to the Catholic Philip of Spain, meant that Catholicism was identified in the public mind with foreign interference and ruthless persecution. Ironically, therefore, a devoted Catholic queen had inflicted long-term damage on her own religion with catastrophic consequences for its followers. The final blow to the Catholic cause was the prolonged conflict with Spain during Elizabeth I's reign which caused Catholics to be perceived as potential traitors to England.

The arrival of King James I on the English throne in 1603 raised Catholic hopes of an easier existence. 'A golden time we have of unexpected freedom,' murmured Father Henry Garnet, the Jesuit Superior in England. This optimism was not entirely misplaced, for James's mother, Mary Queen of Scots, had been Catholic, his wife, Anne of Denmark, had converted to Catholicism and it was rumoured that the king himself was about to do the same. Even the Pope believed this. Both he and his English followers could not have been more wrong.

ABOVE: *Queen Mary I ('Bloody Mary') was one of the most unhappy, despised and least successful of all English monarchs. During her 6-year reign, she executed many Protestants purely on the grounds of their religion.*

LEFT: *John Foxe's 'Book of Martyrs' (1563) luridly describes Queen Mary's savage persecution of Protestants including the horrific burning of so-called heretics at the stake. Foxe's work did much to stir up hatred of Catholicism throughout England.*

ABOVE: *The arrival of King James I proved to be a false dawn for the nation's Catholics as the tolerance he had promised never materialized. James was intelligent but lazy, devious, debauched and thoroughly untrustworthy.*

ABOVE: *Medieval Baddesley Clinton in Warwickshire was a major centre for Catholic recusants, and contains a number of secret hiding places. In 1591 here, nine men, including Father Garnet, stood waist deep in icy water for many hours to evade capture.*

ABOVE: *Coughton Court, near Alcester, Warwickshire, was to have been the HQ of the armed uprising that was to follow the destruction of Parliament. Today, Coughton has a fine museum devoted to the Gunpowder Plot.*

Early in 1604, at an ecclesiastical conference at Hampton Court Palace, James attacked Roman Catholic doctrine. At the new Parliament that year, there was no mention of Catholic toleration. On the contrary, new anti-Catholic legislation was introduced. Fines for 'recusants' (Catholic objectors; see panel below), previously abolished, were reintroduced, and all Jesuits (members of the Society of Jesus, a Catholic missionary order) were ordered to leave the country.

Thus, under James, Roman Catholics increasingly became a minority in England, often marginalized, despised and persecuted. Recusants inhabited a twilight world, worshipping in secret, Mass being conducted by Jesuit priests who crept furtively around the countryside, often hiding from the authorities in elaborately constructed secret rooms known as 'priests' holes'. Recusants were systematically fined and sometimes imprisoned. Jesuits who had ignored the warning to leave, if caught, were executed.

While many Catholics resigned themselves to their fate, others, more militant, were not prepared to do so. Rather, they resolved to resist by any means they thought appropriate, even extreme ones. The stage was set for one of the most dramatic events in English history.

The Plot is Hatched

Robert Catesby, a Catholic activist who had supported the Earl of Essex's attempt to overthrow Queen Elizabeth in 1601, was equally not prepared to accept the situation under her successor. Completely disenchanted with the king's failure to deliver perceived promises of toleration for Roman Catholics, he realized also that the 1604 treaty ending the war between England and Spain meant that Spain would not now support an armed Catholic uprising to overthrow the king and his government.

The solution, Catesby reasoned, lay in Catholics' own hands. Moreover, it must be devastating, dramatic and decisive. In the early spring of 1604 he came up with an answer – to 'blow up Parliament House with gunpowder', thereby destroying the king, his family, nobles, bishops, judiciary and Members of Parliament – the entire English establishment. This audacious plan he confided to his initial trio of conspirators, Tom Winter, Jack Wright and Thomas Percy. 'The nature of the disease requires so sharp a remedy,' he told them.

ABOVE: *Robert Catesby, the leader of the Gunpowder Plot, failed in his objective, yet died a Catholic martyr at the age of 32.*

BELOW: *Chastleton House, Oxfordshire, belonged to Catesby until he was forced to sell in order to pay fines incurred after the abortive Essex Rebellion in 1601. It remains one of the nation's finest Jacobean houses.*

Catesby was extremely handsome with great charm and a magnetic personality. A natural leader, he inspired men to follow him, even when their lives were in peril. Catesby was no stranger to armed insurgency. The huge fine which resulted from his involvement in an abortive coup of 1601 against Elizabeth I compelled him to sell his estate at Chastleton in Oxfordshire, leaving him extremely poor. Fellow conspirator Winter was Catesby's cousin; indeed, most of those involved in the Gunpowder Plot were part of a large, close-knit Midlands family – or were related by marriage. In this respect Winter's Flanders contact,

Guy Fawkes, was an outsider, coming from the north and with no family connections.

Like Guy Fawkes, Catesby and the other plotters saw themselves as brave warriors fighting a holy cause. The blades of their swords were engraved with the words 'the passion of Christ'. In hatching their scheme, they added their names to the long roll of those who have, throughout history, attempted to justify extreme violence in the name of religion.

Unlike many violent activists, Catesby and his colleagues did not come from poor or underprivileged backgrounds. Rather they were young country gentlemen: dashing, good looking, expert swordsmen. Yet, regardless of any romantic image, they were still embarking on a terrible deed.

LEFT: *Guy Fawkes was the only person connected with the Plot whose name is instantly remembered today.*

FAR LEFT: *Thomas Percy, on behalf of the Earl of Northumberland, met James several times before he became king of England and was led to believe that James would favour Catholics. The realization that he had been misled made Percy join the conspirators.*

ACQUIRING EXPLOSIVES
Obtaining gunpowder in early 17th-century England was surprisingly easy, particularly after the war against Spain ended in 1604, when restrictions were relaxed and there was a surplus available. The plotters obtained their powder from the London docks by claiming it was for the English Regiment fighting for Spain in Flanders, which would by then have been a perfectly legal transaction.

The Plot Thickens

O n Sunday 20 May 1604, Guy Fawkes joined Catesby, Winter, Percy and Jack Wright, Percy's brother-in-law, in an upper room of The Duck and Drake, a popular inn near the Strand in London. Here Catesby outlined his plan.

Gunpowder would be placed in a tunnel dug beneath the Palace of Westminster to await the opening of Parliament on 5 November. Fawkes, as the only conspirator with knowledge of explosives, would hide there and, on the king's arrival in the chamber above, light a fuse to ignite the powder – a fuse slow-burning enough to allow him to escape down the nearby River Thames.

With king and Parliament wiped out, an armed revolt would begin in the Midlands. Foreign Catholic reinforcements were also expected. The king's young daughter, Princess Elizabeth, who lived near Warwick, would be kidnapped and placed on the throne as a puppet ruler of a kingdom restored to Catholicism.

Hearing this, Winter was appalled, fearing that if they failed, terrible retribution would follow. But Catesby brought his persuasive charm to bear and the doubting Thomas was reassured. Others proved more enthusiastic. 'Shall we always, gentlemen, talk and never do anything?' exclaimed Thomas Percy. The die was cast. Later, Father John Gerard, an old Jesuit friend of Catesby, held Mass

ABOVE: *The young Princess Elizabeth, daughter of King James I, was unaware that the conspirators intended to place her on the throne as a puppet leader once they had assassinated her father.*

BELOW: *Under cover of darkness, Catesby and Fawkes bring gunpowder to the Houses of Parliament by boat from Catesby's house further up the River Thames.*

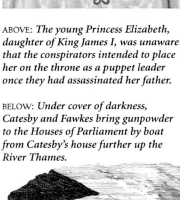

LEFT: *Guy Fawkes lays the powder trail, a skill learned while fighting in Flanders.*

in the next room. Although the priest knew nothing of the plot, he was later to be implicated in it by the authorities.

At first all went smoothly. Gunpowder was bought at the docks and transported upriver to a house in Lambeth. As a Gentleman Pensioner, Percy had the right to live near the Palace of Westminster, and therefore leased a cottage in the area. The plan was to tunnel to the palace. Work began in haste but an outbreak of plague in winter 1604 caused the re-opening of Parliament to be postponed – the date set eventually being 5 November 1605.

Although this allowed longer to penetrate Westminster's medieval walls, the risk of discovery became greater. Moreover, severe digging plus a shortage of money meant a need for more recruits – Kit Wright, Robert Keyes, Thomas Bates, Robert Winter, John Grant, Ambrose Rookwood, Sir Everard Digby and Francis Tresham joined, the number reaching an inauspicious thirteen. Unbeknown to them, their fears of discovery had already been realized.

By spring 1605, the walls threatened to defeat them, but a cellar directly beneath Parliament fortuitously became available. So 20 more barrels of gunpowder were rowed across the river to be stowed there, hidden beneath iron bars, stones and faggots. During summer several further barrels were added.

A PIECE OF GOOD FORTUNE?
The availability of the cellar beneath Parliament might be said to be suspiciously convenient – there is a theory that the wily Earl of Salisbury, by then aware of the plot, made the cellar available in order to catch the plotters red-handed.

LEFT: *The conspirators' London. At the time London Bridge was the only bridge over the Thames, from the rapidly developing south bank to the densely populated ancient City of London.*

Moral Dilemma

The extra months of waiting gave the conspirators time to consider more fully the implications of their scheme: a considerable number of innocent victims would die – the king's wife and children; Roman Catholic peers such as Lord Monteagle (who was the brother-in-law of newly-joined conspirator Francis Tresham); sympathizers like the Earl of Northumberland, Thomas Percy's employer.

Terrible doubts began to emerge, not least in the mind of the leader Robert Catesby. They first surfaced when he ventured to question the Jesuit priest Father Henry Garnet on the subject of violence involving innocents. Again in the summer of 1605, Catesby raised the topic with Garnet. Finally, he confessed his scheme to another Jesuit priest, Father Oswald Tesimond.

With Catesby's permission, Tesimond relayed the information to Father Garnet, who was horrified. Under the strict rules governing confessional, Garnet was forbidden to divulge his terrible knowledge to anyone, something which, understandably, caused him considerable anguish. 'I wish to God I had never heard of the Powder Treason [as the Plot was soon to be called],' he cried some eight months later, by which time he had been implicated and was imprisoned in the Tower of London.

ABOVE: *A contemporary print showing eight of the most prominent plotters. All were destined to die shortly afterwards, and are now virtually forgotten except for Guy Fawkes.*

ABOVE: *The Jesuit priest Henry Garnet was one of a number of innocent people caught up in the Gunpowder Plot. He was destined to pay a terrible price when later publicly executed.*

ABOVE: *William Parker, the 4th Baron Monteagle, brother-in-law of conspirator Francis Tresham. One of the more sinister figures involved in the Gunpowder Plot, he was instrumental in the capture of the plotters, more for himself than for his country.*

Guido Fawkes · Robert Catesby · Thomas Winter

confronted him. However, Tresham was able to persuade Catesby of his innocence.

Did Monteagle, a Catholic who had previously been involved with the Essex Rebellion, fake the letter in order to avoid suspicion of his own involvement with the Plot and ingratiate himself with Salisbury?

Did Salisbury himself write it? There is a theory – far-fetched, perhaps – that he concocted the entire Plot in order to disgrace Roman Catholics completely. Nobody knows, but the idea seems unlikely. What is certain is that the letter sealed the conspirators' fate, particularly that of Guy Fawkes. Salisbury's spies had previously heard vague details of the Plot – but now they had a time and place. The net was fast closing in; the hunters had become the hunted.

On 26 October 1605, with the opening of Parliament now imminent, a curious incident occurred which has never been satisfactorily explained and which remains the subject of controversy. Under cover of darkness, a stranger accosted Lord Monteagle's servant, Thomas Ward, and thrust a letter into his hand warning his master not to attend the coming Parliament – 'as they shall receive a terrible blow.' Monteagle promptly took the letter to the Earl of Salisbury.

Who was the author of this anonymous letter? When Monteagle's servant informed Catesby about it, he immediately suspected Francis Tresham, and angrily

ABOVE: *A fanciful illustration showing the celebrated 'Monteagle letter' being conveyed to King James by an eagle. The letter's origins and authenticity form one of the great unsolved mysteries of the Gunpowder Plot.*

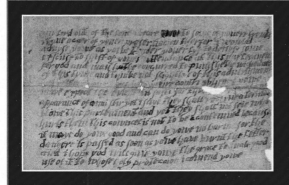

THE MONTEAGLE LETTER
Today, the original of 'this dark and doubtful letter', as it later came to be known, lies in the National Archives at Kew and can be seen on request. Monteagle's servant, Thomas Ward, had connections with Yorkshire Catholics, including the Wright brothers, yet how did he know that Catesby was the leader of the Plot? Had Catesby tried to recruit one too many potential conspirators, or was some other information network involved?

Countdown to Zero Hour

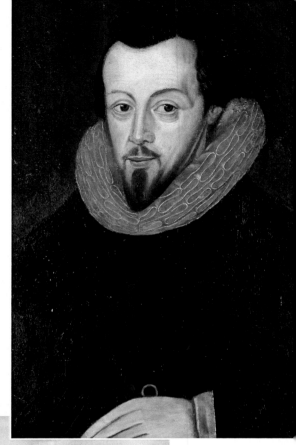

The king was away hunting in the country when the Earl of Salisbury first saw the Monteagle letter. Salisbury, 'that proud and terrible dwarf', now knew he could orchestrate events with his customary masterly precision. Deciding not to inform King James for the time being, he busied himself like a spider spinning an ever larger web, gathering evidence for the inevitable show trial that would follow the capture of the conspirators. He ordered a search of the Parliament cellars, 'but not until the traitors might not be scared before they had let the manner run unto a full ripeness'.

At this point it would have seemed eminently prudent to abort the Plot or at least postpone it, as several of the plotters advised, knowing that Salisbury now possessed the Monteagle letter and had wind of their intentions. Yet Catesby was not a prudent man and, having overcome his doubts, was so focused on executing his plan that he refused to heed any caution. The Gunpowder Plot had become an obsession, to be completed against all the odds and at any cost.

Meanwhile Sir Everard Digby, Robert Winter and other conspirators responsible for organizing the intended uprising in the Midlands, galloped energetically around the countryside gathering additional horses and arranging secret caches of arms and ammunition ready for immediate use. At the same time they tried to enlist additional support

ABOVE: *Robert Cecil, Earl of Salisbury, ran an elaborate network of spies and informers. Thus he was able to detect the Gunpowder Plot at an early stage – and act accordingly.*

LEFT: *Hatfield House, Hertfordshire, was given to Salisbury by King James. It is still owned by the Salisbury family and contains many original 17th-century documents relating to the Gunpowder Plot.*

LEFT: *Guy Fawkes was crucial to the Plot, being the only conspirator capable of handling gunpowder.*

a Piece of good underplot

ABOVE: *Ashby St Legers, Midlands home of Sir William and Lady Anne Catesby, Robert's parents, was reputedly one of a number of locations used by the conspirators when planning the Gunpowder Plot. The gatehouse, shown here, is known as the Plot House.*

ABOVE: *Guy Fawkes's lantern was presented to the Ashmolean Museum, Oxford, by a descendant of one of those who had arrested Fawkes in the cellars.*

from influential local Catholics but were met with a disappointingly lukewarm response. Most of those approached did not favour such violent proposals and were fearful of the reprisals which might ensue. At the same time the plotters were extremely conscious that the more people they told, the greater the risk of betrayal, discovery and the inevitable, gruesome, fate. With no news of how things were going in the capital, their confidence began to wane and their tension to grow.

In the meantime, in the swirling November fog of Jacobean London, Catesby and other conspirators such as Percy and Tom Winter crept furtively around dark alleyways, watching and waiting. Fawkes, having checked his barrels a few days before, began on 3 November his solitary sojourn. In the gloomy, clammy, claustrophobic atmosphere of the cellar below the House of Lords, he counted down the hours and minutes, awaiting the moment when he could light the powder train and escape down the river to a waiting ship for Flanders, and safety.

King James was obsessed with his own safety. He had a morbid fear of assassination and especially of explosions, since his father, Lord Darnley, had been blown up by gunpowder. When James was finally told of the Plot on 1 November 1605, he was enraged. Salisbury, in contrast, remained calm; now was the time for him to carry out his plan.

On his instructions, Sir Thomas Knevett, a Justice of the Peace for Westminster, led a group of Yeomen of the Guard to search the palace cellars. In the small hours of 5 November, they discovered 'a very tall and desperate fellow', clad in a swirling cloak and tall hat, lurking alone in a vault below the House of Lords with a lantern, a watch, slow-burning matches and touchwood, barrels of gunpowder all around him.

Fawkes was immediately challenged, arrested and hustled away for questioning. He said nothing beyond giving a false name – John Johnson. The following day Parliament met briefly. In the margin of the Commons Journal, the Clerk, Ralph Evans, made the following note: 'This last Night the Upper House of Parliament was searched by Sir Thomas Knevett; and one Johnson, Servant to Mr Thomas Percy, was there apprehended; who had placed 36 Barrels of Gunpowder in the Vault under the House with a Purpose to blow the King, and the whole company, when they should there assemble. Afterwards divers other Gentlemen were discovered to be of the Plot.'

The arrest of Guy Fawkes in the cellar below the House of Lords together with 36 barrels of gunpowder – said to be enough to destroy Parliament 20 times over.

The Gunpowder Plot, one of the greatest threats to state security that the nation has ever experienced, had failed. King James, Parliament and the nation had been spared. By then all London was buzzing with wild rumours, and the conspirators in the capital began to fear the worst. Their fears were confirmed when Winter overheard an excited comment that 'there is a treason discovered in which King and Lords were to have been blown up'. The conspirators fled on horseback to join their colleagues in the Midlands, bearing the grim news 'Mr Fawkes is taken and the whole plot discovered'.

On further examination, the king's men realized that the gunpowder was decayed and would never have ignited. Did Salisbury know this already by some subtle means? It would seem that the conspirators were incapable of getting anything right. 'The Powder Treason' had proved an abject failure, yet was destined to cause English Catholics considerable hardship for generations to come.

ABOVE: *A Victorian painting of Guy Fawkes brought before King James for interrogation. The king is said to have been impressed by the calm demeanour of the prisoner. When James asked if he had any regrets, Fawkes replied, 'Only that I have failed to kill the king'.*

Torture in the Tower

As Guy Fawkes began his sojourn in the Tower of London, the rest of the plotters gathered in the Midlands. Urged on by Catesby, they were, amazingly, still determined to press ahead with an armed uprising. When that proved futile they fled, for a last desperate stand, to Holbeach House in Staffordshire, owned by Stephen Littlejohn, one of their rapidly diminishing group of supporters.

Catesby and his bedraggled, exhausted companions arrived there late on 7 November. Unwisely, they attempted to dry gunpowder in front of a fire! The inevitable explosion happened, injuring Catesby and Rookwood and blinding John Grant. Ironically, those who wanted to blow up Parliament had only succeeded in injuring themselves.

The following morning Holbeach House was besieged by Sir Richard Walsh, High Sheriff of Worcestershire, and a large posse of heavily-armed men. The Wright brothers and Thomas Percy were shot and killed. Catesby, badly wounded, crawled into the house and was later found dead, clutching a picture of the Virgin Mary. Winter, Rookwood and Grant were captured. Other arrests followed.

Fawkes, meanwhile, had been thrust into the infamous cell in the Tower known as 'Little Ease', its occupant scarcely having room to sit down. He persisted with the name Johnson, admitting little else, least of all the names of his co-conspirators. The king, in attendance, ordered torture. 'The gentler tortures are first to be used unto him and so by degrees to the worst – and so God speed your good work,' he commanded. Fawkes was taken to the gloomy underground chamber beneath the White Tower, where the 'gentler tortures' began – he was hung from a wall by manacled wrists for hours on end. By remaining silent, he qualified for the 'worst' tortures. For him this meant the rack, whereby victims were tied hand and foot, on their back, to a wooden frame, then slowly stretched until their limbs were dislocated. Often the mere sight of this fearful apparatus induced a confession.

Fawkes, however, endured two days and nights of excruciating pain, but inevitably his resistance eventually failed. He confessed his name and the names of some of the people involved including Father Gerard and Francis Tresham, who was himself brought to the Tower – perhaps poetic justice, as it is suspected that he had informed against fellow plotters. Tresham, however, was ill and died before he could be brought to trial.

The Tower of London housed many high-profile political prisoners in the 17th century.

LEFT: *Condemned plotters are placed on hurdles, to be dragged by horses to the place of execution.*

BELOW: *The rack was singularly effective in extracting confessions. Few could bear the excruciating pain it caused and victims often sustained permanent injury.*

ABOVE: *Signatures of Guy Fawkes, before and after torture, show the ordeal he had endured in the Tower of London. The original signatures are kept in the National Archives at Kew.*

ART IMITATES LIFE

Fact and fiction became intertwined in the plays that William Shakespeare was writing around the same time. *Othello* (1603), *King Lear* (1605) and *Macbeth* (1606) are tragedies exploring the same themes – intrigue, treachery and violent death – acted out for real in the gloomy events of the time. They were performed at the Globe Theatre, now superbly recreated close to the original site on the south bank of the River Thames in London.

Trial and Retribution

The trial began on a bitterly cold January morning in Westminster Hall, scene of many dramatic state trials. The room was packed with spectators including the king, who watched discreetly from behind a curtain.

Fawkes pleaded not guilty – which was surprising as he had previously admitted his intentions and his lack of remorse. All the others did likewise except Digby. Inevitably, each of them was condemned and sentenced to be hanged, drawn and quartered; that is, the convicted man was hanged by the neck, cut down while still alive, his entrails torn out then his body hacked into four bloody pieces, usually then to be prominently displayed.

Guy Fawkes was the last to be executed, having been dragged through the streets past huge crowds to a scaffold erected in Old Palace Yard, Westminster, adjacent to the building he had failed to destroy.

The hunt for traitors did not end with the deaths of the plotters, as the ruthless Salisbury was determined to prove Jesuit involvement. Under torture Thomas Bates had implicated Gerard and Tesimond. Both men managed to escape to the Continent but Father Garnet was captured and taken to the Tower where in May 1606, after torture and trial, he too was hanged, drawn and quartered.

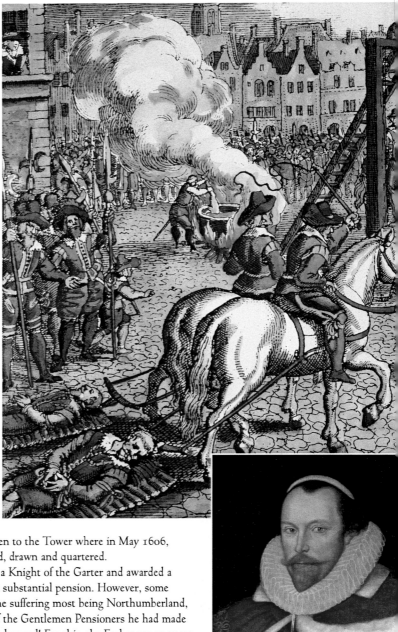

The triumphant Salisbury was made a Knight of the Garter and awarded a magnificent estate. Monteagle received a substantial pension. However, some Catholic peers were heavily fined, the one suffering most being Northumberland, Thomas Percy's employer; as Captain of the Gentlemen Pensioners he had made Percy a Pensioner – part of the king's bodyguard! For this, the Earl spent 17 years in the Tower.

A wave of anti-Catholic feeling swept across England, and for a long time 5 November was the signal for anti-Catholic riots. Repressive laws followed. Catholics were banned from the legal profession and from any form of government service, including becoming officers in the armed services. Many of these restrictions lasted well into the 19th century and even today a monarch cannot be a Catholic or marry into that faith.

ABOVE: *Sir Edward Coke, the Attorney General, led the case for the prosecution with a clear remit to demonstrate beyond doubt the guilt and evil of the plotters.*

WESTMINSTER HALL

The largest surviving part of the ancient Palace of Westminster was built 1097–99 for William II. Most of the rest was destroyed by fire in 1834. Richard II raised the walls and installed the magnificent single-span hammer-beam roof, the longest (c.70 metres; 230 feet) timber roof in Europe, and one of the oldest. Although tennis balls dating back to the time of Henry VIII have been found in its rafters, the hall is chiefly famous for the trials that once took place here – including those of Sir Thomas More, King Charles I and Guy Fawkes. More recently the bodies of George V, George VI, Sir Winston Churchill and HM Queen Elizabeth, the Queen Mother, lay in state here.

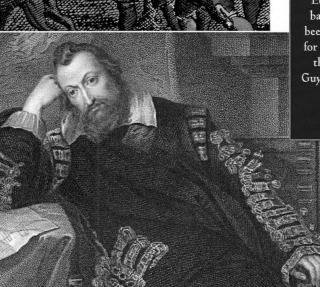

ABOVE LEFT: *The condemned plotters were dragged through crowded streets en route to their execution. They were hanged, drawn and quartered, a traditional penalty for traitors.*

LEFT: *Henry Percy, Earl of Northumberland, was the kinsman and employer of Thomas Percy, who had visited the earl at Syon House, his London home, the day before the Plot was discovered. He was fined a huge sum of money and imprisoned in the Tower.*

19

Continuing Traditions

The legacy of Guy Fawkes lingers into the 21st century. Four hundred years after his abortive attempt to blow up the Houses of Parliament, he remains one of the best known of the nation's historical figures. Each year before the State Opening of Parliament the cellars under the Palace of Westminster are searched by the Yeomen of the Guard. Today this is largely a ceremonial event, but not out of keeping with the vigilance which still remains necessary.

The first bonfires to celebrate the capture of Guy Fawkes were lit shortly after the discovery of the Plot in 1605. Four centuries later 5 November is still known as 'Bonfire Night' throughout the nation, and is often accompanied by the ceremonial burning of an effigy of Guy Fawkes. This tradition even crossed the Atlantic to America as 'Pope Day', when the burning of an effigy of the Pope, together with unpopular politicians, also took place on 5 November, mainly in former British colonies on the eastern seaboard.

Sir William Waad, the Lieutenant Governor of the Tower of London during the early 17th century, erected an elaborate monument to the discovery of the Gunpowder Plot at the Tower which remains to this day, as indeed do the Bloody Tower and the White Tower, where the luckless Fawkes lived out his last few months before his execution at the age of only 36. Today his memory, very literally, continues to burn brightly.

On Bonfire Night, every 5 November, effigies of Guy Fawkes are ceremonially burned throughout the nation, one of the few ceremonies that Cromwell allowed to continue during the time that England was a republic.

RIGHT: *By tradition, the Yeomen of the Guard (or 'Beefeaters') still search the cellars of Parliament the night before the State Opening.*

OPPOSITE: *'Penny for the guy?' is a traditional way for children to make money to buy fireworks for Bonfire Night.*